Perspectives

by R. Martin Basden

Englewood, NJ

ISBN 978-1-936373-55-0

Published in the United States by Unbound Content, LLC, Englewood, NJ.
Cover art: ©2019, by Katherine Hanna

****

Perspectives
First edition 2019

To my bride, Kay, for her loving encouragement and boundless support of my interests. To Nancy Kay Middleton, who guided me to Dr. Robert Christin, founder of a gifted group of poets.
To those poets, The Albrights, who took me in, shared critique salons, encouraged me to submit, and greatly improved my work. Finally, to my publisher, Annmarie Lockhart, without whom this book could not have been accomplished.
Thank you.

Table of Contents

A Likeness

From a distance
I am the familiar stranger
often seen at this crossroads
holding a scribbled sign
you cannot read
you need not read
to understand

Close your window when I approach
check the doors locked
shuffle the contents of your bag
as though something important
requires your immediate attention
and don't look up
until I'm gone
that you might escape
the fear that you and I
tread bare the same pathway

Green Persimmons

On a summer visit to Georgia
just old enough to be on my own
not big enough to do much of anything on the farm
except collect eggs
pick vegetables for Granny
or fetch the bamboo fishing poles for Grandpa

One of those hot days when
plowing was out of the question
Grandpa told me to get the poles
He got the bloodworms from the ice-box
strode off down the back pasture toward his pond

I got hung up in barbed wire
said something no ten year old should utter
He stood in the persimmon orchard inquiring of my wounds
I said something worse

He said what I needed was in the tree
motioned for me to climb
pointed to a yellow fruit
I thought it was medicine for my scratches
He told me to take a bite
I wondered if I should rub it on my wounds
He held his hand to mimic taking a bite
I did
and discovered that he was treating my vocabulary
Persimmons do not ripen before a frost
when the alum turns sweet

I Disturbed a Guppy Grave

I disturbed a Guppy grave
in the flower garden soil
half of what looked like
a small ceramic lighthouse
turquoise fish-tank gravel
remnants of frilly plastic
but no miniature bones

I said a child's prayer
just in case

R. Martin Basden

Live Oaks on a July Morning

I am the supple maple sapling
whose playful leaves
flutter in a light breeze
while live oak companions
seem not to notice morning gusts

and by my movement
among this hundred year landscape
whisper a message
that before I was born
before you were born
here stood grandeur
in a pose no different
than today

Mom in Her Hostess Apron

As gracious as the word, she cares for everyone
as though they are guests.
Even the dog is treated with the same snacks
that Mom would eat.
Not so bad for hot dogs or rice,
not so good for chocolate
or other harmful or indigestibles for canines.
After the no-no treats, I usually get to clean up ejections
from doggie bowel or jowl.

It is not surprising, that Mom offered a snack
to the housekeeper,
who showed me Mom's offering
of a small silver platter filled
with miniature marshmallows, M&M chocolates,
and dry dog food.

After advising her to toss the treat,
I dashed to the dog bowl
to investigate if chocolate was slipped
into the dog's menu. To my surprise,
not a single marshmallow or M&M candy was in the bowl.
There was, however, a large dollop of grape jelly
atop fresh dry dog food.

I didn't wait for that trial-and-error experiment to play out.

Days of Old Young Images

She fingered photos
from a lidless box
turning one
and another
reading aloud
faded pencil names
 asked me
again who they
were

Blanket Down

Beach sleeping
Totally warm
Licking breezes
Tickling sand
Gull calls
Roaring waves
Almost dreams
Muffled voices
Gritting thumps
Tanning scent
Cold droplets
Breath taking
Raucous laughter
Blinding light
Clearing head
Smiling friends
Game declined
Drift again
Beach sleeping

The Boys of Summer

Heavy woods wade along the marsh edge
where we took measure in spare winter forest
for a whispering place of summer secrets

Five boys under twelve in gray light
scoured shadows of hollow trunk as back room
to a vine cave we would form in the matted twist of
honeysuckle and briars that cover everything in spring
save clearings shorn by machete
and paths smoothed by feet

In the cold of winter we stole into the forest
sculpting side paths to nowhere
dead-end trails to mislead intruders in our camp

As warming days dressed the mazes of our labor
we trimmed open the curving way
to a vista of nothing but reeds amuck
and cattails swaying in a summer breeze
sharpened the turn at a great oak
to a screen of poison ivy
and let briar tendrils disguise the entry of our vault

There we perfected idleness and braggadocio
the commerce of petty liars and young boys
boasting of athletic prowess beyond our physical ability
of sexual conquests with neighborhood girls
before we had the courage to speak with them

Perspectives

21

It was profane and holy

A place where laughter spawned laughter for no reason at all
where strength and trust proved leadership
first cigarettes were smoked
big dreams were shared
where farts were graded
and friendships fed
where my memory walks
in another mid-summer wood

Adolescence

Adolescence was a blur stretching interminably
like a prison for aspirations
bound by inexperience wrapped in indecision
so cautious
so careless
when love erupted

She was new to the neighborhood
made all the girls look like girls
with the pinch of her waist
those metronome hips
the shimmer of her blouse
as she changed her pace

Dark shoulder length hair caressed her face
as I wished my hands could do
The most luscious pouting full lips ever to be painted red
made love to her smile
With but fleeting glance from emerald eyes
I lost my breath

Her name was Teresa Morgan
and I was stung
snagged on the timeless barb of desire

So I plotted a course of conquest
a barrage of words
a poem to show her what I could not tell her
a literary persuasion in place of conversation
that failed me when she looked my way

Perspectives

On a Friday evening I created a masterpiece
of sweet passages of gentleness
strident phrases of musk
humor in innuendo
and pleading

I hadn't told her that I was coming
In fact, I do not remember having spoken with her at all

Saturday found me walking to her house
paper folded and sticking to my palm
I stood on the public sidewalk outside her gate
and waited
pretending not to be there

Soon Teresa emerged and seemed to float toward me
smiling that heart-stopping smile
hair bouncing flawless in waves
and eyes focused on the note
nested in my upturned trembling hand

All movement slowed
all sound abated but the pounding of my heart

Two delicate fingers lifted the folded sheet
barely touching either side as she examined
the wordless exterior
I didn't have to hear the "NO"
formed silently by her lips

I stood naked in rejection as the crumpled unread note
carried my countenance to concrete

Finals

I was worried about
that entrance test for heaven
until
GOD told me it's
an open book exam

Now
 I'm really worried

Kites

A glimpse of eternity visited me yesterday.
Souls posing as kites filled a summer sky.
Swatches of color loosed from visceral clutch,
were carried on gentle air from horizon to horizon.
Some were patterned, others plain, all seemed to float with
purpose.
In clusters of three and parties of twelve, they kept company.
Occasionally one would slide from its group, tag another,
and the two would dance a swirling round of sharing.
I smiled
as the calico grandmother cavorted
with the yellow stillborn.

Siesta

Sometime between one and four on certain afternoons
I find the luxury of a nap irresistible
To slide down in the chair and find that neutral point
where all stretched out I'm neither seated nor supine
I close my eyes and fade into my own breath
drift through dialogue with no one
about subjects I never knew I knew
wake as at new beginning
to rejoin whatever it was
that I wasn't doing
when I left

That First Kiss

That first kiss
was just a pinpoint
on the map of life,
but oh, so, vital.

Teetering between want and consequence,
it was
hesitant,
awkward,
done
in a delicious mix
of haste and dwell.

Another Morning

Another morning offers a nature call
to the dog and for me
a chance to watch the half-moon's wan smile
above the horizon
taunt sunrise from darkness with a
catch me if you can
borrowed primacy.

Or is it boredom's reflection
of endless repetition
on her pale surface
in the *which chases what* rigor of pursuit
that I can witness
at the cusp
of any new day?

From the Tree I Used to Climb

Now that I can whittle on dried branches
having no particular employ to attend
my mind wanders from the pile of chips
dry and fragile at my feet to the tree
whose limb this used to be

It bore twigs and leaves
funneled sap to sunlight
chlorophyll to root
thickened ring by ring
to be this stick about to become
a walking aid for aged legs
once fit to climb and hang
from just such a limb

Branching Out

Oh! to be wild and free
snuggled up to some honey of a birch
in a secluded wood
But Nooo!
A landscaper wannabe stuck me
and my siblings single file in
scant five feet of dirt between
bus route and playground
tagged me with my sister's name Pink Myrtle
when it's plain to see I'm a male
Just look at these branches
all knotted and swelled
a real tree guy would know
but I got even
held my breath for two weeks
turned red

Oh! To smell pine and feel again
the prickle of falling needles
on my bare limbs in winter
But Nooo!
I get year-round doses of diesel exhaust
unbelievable scents from the bodies of
playground ruffians scraping their curiosity
in my convenient crotches
dogs who leave gifts at the altar of my roots
cats who scratch where I do not itch
and natural though it may be
I can't wait for the rain to wash my foliage free
of bird poop

Oh! To be anywhere but here
where birds taunt me with hints
of beauty beyond my sight
But Nooo!
Closest I get to sunrise is a billboard
advertising orange juice
sunset is a rumor behind tall bricks
my river a gutter after hard rain
Closest I get to fun is
drooping a limb at passersby
and dropping seed pods
as captivity protest

Oh! To grow tall as my ancestors
to surround my waist with slender shoots
which are my children
But Nooo!
Just before the rush of spring
fatherless children of groundskeepers come
trim my natural beauty limb by limb stubby
butcher the young ones at my feet
make uniform the row of sisters and brothers
like giant fluff-less dandelions waiting
the summer fullness of supple new growth
wanting the precious brush
of familial contact caused
by a breeze

Oh! To be wild and free

Aroma Therapy

Sit alone in quiet isolation, with folded hands in your lap.
Eyes closed and chin on your chest, do nothing for a while.

Then, smell the past.

Bacon cooking downstairs
Honeysuckle on the fence
Spilled Clorox bleach
Musk on the nape in the back seat
Buttered popcorn in the theatre
Dog poop on your shoe
Freshly washed clothes
Newly plowed soil
Incense in a dark room
Dead skunk on the roadside
The air after rain
Mom's fingernail polish remover
Full diaper anywhere nearby
Coconut oil at the beach
Your lover's hair in the dark
Tennis shoes in the locker
Sleeping baby's cheek next to yours
New paint on the walls
Rain wet dog
Roses in full bloom

Your own home after a trip
Very old kitty litter
Gardenias outside an open window
Steak on the grill
Vomit in the car
Chimney smoke in the neighborhood
Hot cinnamon cider with cloves on the stove
Rotting fish at the shore
Fresh cut pine limbs
Hot sweaty sex
Fresh coffee brewing

How was your trip?

R. Martin Basden

Forests Give It Up

There was no sound without the wood,
but one could hear a symphony within.

The thunk, thunk, thunk of beak to bark
as grub-hungry pecker sought repast.
Whoop, whoop, whoop gave counterpoint,
from unseen cousin beyond a distant ridge.
Songbirds pushed melodious rips
from branch to branch, as Jays played tags
like bursts of tenor sax.

And there I stood,
Immersed,
in a repeat performance
of original surround sound.

Hidden by the Light

5 AM at the foot of the drive
a cardboard box
last occupied by sixteen rolls of paper towels
slipped easily over my shoulders
blocked out all the surrounding pre-dawn neighborhood
lights
and through its open bottom
revealed hundreds of brilliant stars
in the dark canopy of a cloudless sky

R. Martin Basden

I Had to Read It Again

The memorable poem
was constructed with numerous shelves
offering me a plentiful selection of familiars
disguised in slanted perspective
a change in rhythm
cacophony pummeling calm
the taste of alum when sugar was expected
bare spaces where adjectives whispered hints
of their departure
invitations to pause
ruminate
desire
to read again

Image

Posted as fact
in the physiology course
Far more muscles form a frown
than a smile
I have been told that I have
a strong face

Look! Over There!

It is not for lack of things to do
that little seems accomplished
but the capital I as in interruption
which whisks me from intent
to a side step
on a lesser path
an intrusion upon that first clear want
suddenly diminished
by an irresistible urge to deviate
toward the incomplete
the out of place
the glaring triangle among squares
and make it fit where it does not

Oh the I
the I
I want to conquer
gone astray

Mizzu

A show-me breeze arrived yesterday
and fluffed up shared memories
of lost gifts and daily rites

Comfortable would best describe our time
splitting beans and sipping drinks
to toast renewed acquaintance

Hours spent stitching a verbal quilt
sewing generations past and present
to meld old swatches to new patterns

A show-me breeze left today
sauntering too soon on the path
which passes both our doors

R. Martin Basden

Origin

They ask me how ideas come

They smile and wait for an answer

I search for a clue
that hints what meal
taken half a century ago with
Chaucer at Canterbury
Milton in Paradise or
E. Dickinson at tea
what glimpse of children
what puff of smoke
what sarcasm suffered
has ruminated long enough to become
a poem
I smile and tell them
what they want to hear

Monk's Breakfast

Vow of silence the order of morning
gives form to the ritual of preparation

Stout blade halves stiff bagel
butter falls like whittled wood chips
and wait their fate on the wheat altar
Cold black to searing orange relaxes the curls
to form shimmering golden puddles
on a plateau of browning crisp

Rescued from the heat and dressed
with a cool filet of cream cheese
an offering is given to break the fast

Crescent bite of crunch and squeeze
pushed against chamber roof
chewed rolled mixed savored
swallowed bit after bit
until tongue scours the mouth
sweeps crevices for flavor
polishes teeth and pats the pallet

Final taste rinsed with a gulp of air
and silent Ahhhh

R. Martin Basden

Recovery

He fell from that ladder
broke his shoulder and wrist
cleaning the gutters
clearing a Saturday list
for me

Sunday rest is what he must
but asks for his guitar
and with my help
straps it to his chest
fingers the frets
while I stand behind him
and pluck out
his favorite tunes

Return to Sender

Child
I left you jump-roping on the front walk
pigtails bouncing
bowed head over bowed body chanting
sing-song solo to the measure of each spin
words I can't remember
in a voice I won't forget   fresh
as the ink on this post card
a plaintive daughter   calling me
home

Away to the Garden

Away to the garden my refuge of choice
from concerns of debt and finance
confrontation and schedules

Safe haven where soil between fingers
soothes the turmoil in my brain
quiets the chatter of conscience
where burdens of responsibility are lost
in the monoculture of sand and clay and loam
and a cleansing of soul is propagated
where I kneel

Wordsmith

She called me wordsmith
and the image of muscular forearm poised in mid strike
fist grasping handle in a backdrop of flame and sparks
flashed to my imagination
took form in the work
hammering long phrases into small spaces
dwelt there a while until thoughts
quenched themselves in the cooling spray of quiet
comforted
calmed
to become
the hardened steel
of love words

What Draws the Eye

Amidst a flow of daffodils and jonquils
a splash of iridescent pink in sunlight
tulips
anchoring a turn
of ubiquitous pastels
trouping off to shade

Upkeep Can't Keep Up

They're like ants these tourists
like ants that come in the warm weather
to tote off my place one stone at a time

The new stones added
in winter's desolation
chosen in the distant quarry
shaped for each hollow spot
hundreds up the hill
hundreds by the satchel
heavy on the shoulder
gone by summer's end
souvenirs in picnic baskets

R. Martin Basden

Prevarication

Tossing lies around like
air filled balloons
rushing to keep them airborne
keep them airborne
so they do not touch down
to burst
and expose their insides

Balancing half-truths like
spinning plates on vertical sticks
rushing to keep them spinning
keep them spinning
so they do not fall
to shatter
and destroy their usefulness

Pass It On

Come naked once again
in give and take
of tenderness.

Lie down here and shed
this day's worries
so heavy.

Let fingertips trace
uncharted outlines
upon you.

Pass the night in peace
found only by
loves's balm.

Greet the morning smiling,
full again of gifts
to give.

Ssenippah

Everybody knows when it's gone.
Not one soul or vast congregation
can really tell you how to find it.
It's personalized.
It's paradoxically singular and multiply complex.
Tinted by sight, taste, hearing, touch, and smell;
circumstance, occurrence, and experience border it.
Sensed more during absence, it's usually,
only fully appreciated in the past tense.
Often, you have to see it backward
to know it was yours.

More to It

"I can't do this",
"I'd never try that",
are easy mantras for we nestled comfortable
in the cocoon of self-limitation.

Never challenged, never hurt.
We trade the blade of opportunity
for the handle of control
and wait bloodless
for change that never comes.

The shadow of an image formed shallow in the mind
explodes vertical by light cast upon the profile,
startles those of us who think we know our own boundaries,
startles us to think
we could be more.

To stay the historical course is an easy, effortless, death.
To taste the salty tincture of conflict
is to live.

R. Martin Basden

Learn to Shoot Your Dog

He said it to me on several occasions
when he was sixty-something
old by the standards of a pre-teen

I thought I understood
the images clear to me now as then

Put down that lame mule
ease the torture from a mangled leg
suffered in a fall in the gully out back

End the misery so clear in his eyes
of the dog hit by a car that never stopped

Smother the calf born with no abdominal wall

But it was later
when the lesson took real meaning in my life

Turn from those who would cheat another
silence the back-stabber
do not traffic with liars

Forgive once
avoid twice

From the Loft of Experience

Watch from the parapets of parenthood
the never casual evolution of children

From the loft of experience see youth
whose vision flat and side to side
commit to pitfall and prank
with gleeful disconnect
of cause and effect

Wince and wonder as they wrestle
with whether words blindly purchased
with peer currency

Hope and pray your voice
is more to them
than tinnitus

R. Martin Basden

Circle

Smiles in the Joy of Love
Joy in the Love of Peace
Love in the Peace of Smiles
Peace in the Smiles of Joy

Brevity

In my youth,
I swallowed the April moon,
traced the Big Dipper along the curve
of a summer lover's body,
hung promises on a morning star,
gave time a farewell kiss.

A stranger to the dark canopy for decades,
I look at it differently in these later years.

Now on sleepless nights,
I ponder brevity revealed in the silent sky.
That barely visible smudge above us
a galaxy long ago,
bursting its expiration notice
a million light years away.

Its absence calls me
to waste not seconds in anger,
love more passionately
in this cosmic instant we share

Quiet Intersection

Her elbow rested on the driver's window sill
wrist palm-up as if to catch something
the two first fingers and thumb holding
an imaginary cigarette
head bowed in contemplation
as I stared across the lane
blond highlights
in auburn hair rippling
in a light breeze
a moment
before the light changed
eyelids fluttered
head turned
returned my gaze
smiled
left

Senior Travelogue

They say you make life's journey by yourself, and I guess that's true.

I've been to lots of places, but never in Cahoots. Apparently, you can't go alone. You have to be in Cahoots with someone, and I have issues about going to a new place with strangers.

I don't think I've been in Cognito either. I hear nobody recognizes you there, so why bother?

I have, however been in Sane. They don't have an airport; you have to be driven there, and thanks to friends and family, I've made several trips. These are the same people who tell me that I've often been in Considerate, but I have no memory of that.

I'm pretty sure that I've been in Discrete, but they say what happens there stays there, and I hope it's true.

My journey seems to have been mostly in Decision, questioning whether to be in Credible or in Corrigible.

Sometimes, I think I'd like to go to Conclusions, but you usually have to jump to get there. At my age, I'm lucky to get a good walk going.

So, for now, I'll reside in Dulgent, and commune with folks in Ebriated.

When Given a Life Sentence
on the day given diagnosis of acute bone marrow cancer

For me it's a challenge of finding balance for self indulgence, consideration of others, and those necessary responsibilities of health and finance required to form a living.

A daily rebirth of spirit, gratefulness, thanks to God, appreciation of spouse, family and loving friends, is paramount in the maintenance of walls momentarily breached.

To endeavor to be positive with purpose is made easier by a life-long attitude of giving and the sure realization that legacy evidences itself in the faces and words of encouragement of those I must have touched.

Now I have time to do better that which I should have done well all along.

I'd Sooner Wake

I've never had a dream confront me so
with bits of unrelated stuff

Faces familiar unnamed
leftovers from disparate times
in current attire stuck together
like chain links rattling discontent
for having been summoned to now
for a purpose as vague to them as me

A stack of good intentions spread out like playing cards
slip over the edge of a tilted surface into blackness
moan the subject of their creation to their author
as one by one they tumble out of earshot

Just beyond reach
magic wraps the wants and needs of yesterday
in a shadow rag of tomorrow which
flutters at the edge to tease me with a glimpse
ankle and calf without a flash of buttocks
green of cash without denomination
frustration without fulfillment

I'd sooner wake than this

R. Martin Basden

Driving the Eastern Shore

Haze blurs tree-lines
softens landscapes
sets the mood for traveling
unhurried after the funeral
away from clusters of family
whose recent days were seamless
swatches of tears and laughter
talking of the past
mute to the future hollow
with the loss of a beloved

South along the same route
somehow shorter toward home
I notice a man sitting on a dusty suitcase
and ponder who has the better place

I Have No Memory of Love
For my Bride, Kay

I have no memory of Love
No memory of peace
But the harbor of your arms
And the shelter given daily
In your smile

Time does not exist without you by my side
Even time before the vows
That marked us one before the world
Isn't measured isn't meaningful
In its nakedness

For I am clothed in you
Even named as you
As a couplet in a poem
Cannot stand on just one line
There is no me without you
To make the whole

Clean Slate

Waiting for sunrise at a ritual place
as wrinkles of darkness glow with a hint
that the moment is near
when a burning curve will blossom
beneath an awning of clouds
spill itself
toward this spot
warm my face and heart
and burn yesterday's sorrows
in the promise of new beginnings

A Meal at Bob's Poetry Kitchen

*In celebration of Robert Christin, Mentor to we who call
ourselves Albright Poets, in his honor*

Of course, we begin with an aperitif of friendship to
complement canapés spread with shared moments, tart and
delicious. Sometimes sips become drafts to quench a
palliative need.

Appetizers of avant-garde creations are often served by
the host. Whether presented chilled in a gelatin of flavored
ambiguity, or steaming in a fluff of passion, they are skillfully
chosen to whet the appetite for the entrée.

The specialty of the house is encouragement cooked over a
soft critical flame, high enough to seal vitality in, while
cleansing dross from the offering. Two helpings are
recommended.

Flavors abound in side dishes of memoir smothered in a
reminiscence roux, haiku sushi on a bed of pepper-jellied
truth, pastel limerick with an off-color topping, and creamed
humor baked to perfection.

The end of the meal is traditional bitter-sweet parting pie,
always warm, with a drizzle of fresh promise.

Hic!

I like booze
It's a friend who won't bitch if you're late for a meet
and will never complain 'bout your breath
A companion with which you need never compete
and will offer the same 'til your death

What a buddy supreme like it came from a dream
always there
if you've got your check cashed
You can bloody well scream for an Irish mint cream
if you like
you can really get bashed

I like booze
Whether cooled by some ice or fermented from rice
it's warm on the ride going down
It can make you feel nice or some teardrops entice
or give charm to your walk back from town

It can come in a can it can come in a glass
doesn't matter to me one damn bit
just as long as the man by my cup doesn't pass
and the splatter don't fall where I sit
(Hic!)

Madonna

We all know someone
who wears a perpetual closed lip smile
at once comforting and disarming
whose metered response to query
accompanied by a slight tilt of head
or eye movement hesitation
makes one wonder
about what they did not say

Not a matter of veracity
rather a curiosity on our part
that their filtering of word choices could be
softened admonition encouragement or dismissal
which begs a second question some would not ask
for fear of clarification

Forces of Arms

In a God-fearing world and in the absence of God male children raised
to be warriors, invincible images feed more the cast of youngsters at
play in the backyards of war. learning to focus on brutal survival in
the kill-or-be-killed montage of boys at play, living out fantasies again
and again, falling and rising in the romanticism of the game.
We practice the forces of arms.

In the prime of life decisions are made and choices by us or for us are
made, inevitable paths are opened into which we gallantly march or
are blindly herded, leaping from the protected environment of make-
believe at once into harsh reality, leaving the shelter of family and
friends still holding on to the romanticism of the game.
We practice the forces of arms

In the grueling test of sinew, bone, and brawn, the warrior attitude of
boys is exploited; indelicate childhood dreams evolve to become
deadly, employed by more focused men, leaning now on the
organized chaos of teamwork, training, and buddies in kind, lifting
supposedly to unreachable heights, the honor of the romanticism of
the game.
We practice the forces of arms.

In a lottery spin of God's unknown design some are chosen to go and
some left behind, Incredible rush for those sent off to fight, a mix of
adrenaline, humor, and fright, leafing through newsprint of far-away
clashes fails to give balm to men far from harm, lofting their epithets
of hollow displeasure for being deprived of man's ultimate pleasure
to practice the forces of arms.

In hand-to-hand combat or stationed nearby, lobbing their rounds or
bombs from the air, inconceivable horror becomes all too real in the
sacrifice of blood and of soul; listing the many to fall from their
boyhood pursuit and the faceless numerous innocents, losing a friend
or a limb or the virginity of their conscience in the discipline of how
to practice the forces of arms.

In every counted breath of the short-time prophet is a vision of
impending doom, inconvertible images of uncompleted journeys for
those who so valiantly carried on, loving their brothers more than life
and in greater-than-life sacrifices for countrymen, lasting forever
through their deeds in the memory of witnesses soon ambivalent
to practice the forces of arms

In later years which weight men with slower reflexes but wiser steps,
repeated thoughts of humor and horror on certain days sift through,
launching unfettered tears, and now, (just now) laughter from those
who fought and lived; old men turn to whatever God is their God, and
give thanks for safe passage
from the practice of forces of arms

Good Morning

I sense your silent approach
anticipate a fingertip to nape
welcome the chill scampering
across my shoulders
the warmth of your lips

The coffee
can wait

Query Mr. Picasso

Pablo, what were you thinking?
Blue guitarist taking an awkward nap about to be startled angry red
by intrusive fingers at his naked toes intent
on tickling the troubadour out of his blue funk.
No?
Given your predilection for all things sexual,
 it must be a self portrait;
perhaps that breathless half-death after orgasm,
maybe the pangs of disappointment
that both your wife and your lover denied you sweet relief.
Not that?
Then boredom must be the theme,
draining warmth and your passion
for all things creative
filtered through an icy perspective.

Sandy Hook Silence

A photograph of
breathless complaint
thrown heavenward
from gaped mouth conveys
without translation
the rhetoric of pain

That image
seen from our harm free perch
commands our empathetic chorus
cry out
cry out
wail in their stead

On Gray Days

On gray days like this
it's easy to lean into branches of discontent
rough against your back supporting
yet distracting attention from
a nearby touch of balm unnoticed
a plaintive monologue of escape
offering cures for named
and unnamed demons bent
on rending the soul
into irregular pieces
items for critique
in transparent coffin displayed
on a public thoroughfare

At Rest

For Thomas Andrew Hall

"The night sits in this chair."
The opening line of her soliloquy.

"His favorite place to be, to play his strings, to brighten this corner with smiles, or draw you to a quiet tearful sense of relief from your trouble."

"I remember him, joking with friends and siblings, heckling and cajoling some, asking others how he could help in his no-strings-attached way of acceptance without judgement."

"The playful one, wrestling with nieces and nephews, wearing them out, sending them on with pockets full of family imprint. He, in respite to the chair, to read, to study the solution for another's challenge."

"When I close my eyes, I still see him there in the dark. Quiet, thinking, perhaps praying or nodding his head to a tune or his private mantra."

"But, no. The cushion is not pressed with his form. There is no familiar creaking as when he rose to step briskly to a task. He has found a better way to spread his special love, through the thousands he has touched."

"Now, the night sits in this chair."

On Winter's Farm

Along
the highway
stand staggered clumps
of nondescript leafless trees
Huddling naked together as if to find
some shared warmth in crowds
or nestled among their coniferous sisters
for protection from the wind
Rank upon row off the road
hill after valley peopled by them
Some patched together like misfit siblings
others in gangs of mop-headed green or like
strands of stilettos leaning against one another
Bent stoops a trio
clothed only in leafless
kudzu gowns
from foot to brow
and there
near a broken barn
in the open
a single majestic oak
with outstretched arms
so virile so stoic
so utterly alone
stands guard on winter's farm

R. Martin Basden

As If We Could Change Things

As if we could change things
end of life issues weigh heavily
on those who hobble into senior status
count pills more numerous than classmates
spend precious time wishing that
mundane would undress
and usher something startling
to sunrise

instead somewhere
between invincibility and purpose
mortality sneaks up behind you
jerks your pants to your ankles
points
and laughs

On Schedule

Old people like leaves in the forest
change with approaching winter

Some dress themselves in garish
orange yellow red
leap into the arms
of autumn's cooling gusts
in playful confetti departure

A few wave a defiant amber palm
at November's hardy blow

Most simply desiccate
turn brown
wait to be pushed to the next season

Legacy

All of life is a series of decisions
In the swirl of time near the bottom of my life funnel
I vacillate between living in the now
looking at my past
or hurdling decades hence for a peek
Yesterday taps my shoulder whispers in my ear
a reminder of who I have been
Tomorrow hides mute behind two horizons
promises me nothing
waits for me to startle myself with accomplishment
Today I choose to help others
sing my songs
write stories
and try to understand
that this is as close as I am
to tomorrow

The Anchors of Our Lives

The anchors of our lives
are those simple truths
which persist
though we repeatedly
throw them away
surprisingly find them
over and over
dressed in borrowed clothes
slouched in the shadows
of our indiscretions
smiling

Ode to Bob Christin

One can't presume to know
how gratitude is worn by another.
Some feel comfortable slipping into it as a cardigan
on days when bluster swipes
like cold criticism on the shoulders,
or as a cherished bracelet sure to elicit compliment
and the chance to crow about its giver.
Perhaps a special hat
jaunty, rakish, with a feather, will serve.
Whatever the accoutrement,
it will be both reminder and symbol
of the grace you shared with everyone.

I'll wear mine for you like a pair of favorite socks,
every day, and remember your encouragement,
the way you find the germ of life
in dry colorless arrangements of words,
and set a hybrid upon the mantle
above your fireplace.

The Gentle Art

We have lost it
Making lists from our bed of all that is to be done
before close of day
marking off the tasks
racing to complete in the tightest packet of time
each mind consuming assignment
of self-imposed necessity
pouring such urgency into poring over the tab
as we carom from check point to next
that by creeping of sunset
sorry for the short sum of our effort
we are surprised at the lack of energy
the absence of inclination
to simply sit with loved ones
and practice that gentle art
of quiet conversation

I Miss My Poet Friends

Too long away
from gentle counsel and humor of velvet snipe
a would-be bard anxious
for punch or whisper of a recalcitrant muse
leafs through memories of mentors and masters passed
idles in files of finished and unfinished work
suffers each necessary declination to visit
with masters and mentors present
and waits
for an undefined alignment of circumstance
to cast off imaginary restriction
and go play

Age-related Disorder

The rope attached to my six adult decades
feels like an oily knotted cord in my old hands.

The nearest length is cluttered with daily trips around town,
visits to grandchildren, and the usual concerns about the future,
all bobbing up and down like laundry on a clothes-line
as I tug three generations toward me.

Here comes my cancer surgery, fiftieth wedding anniversary,
retirement party, the new house, moving like caterpillars to the taut
and slack of rhythm provided by burning forearms straining to
invert time. My shoulders ache as knot by knot the backward years
come into view.

The next cluster contains the empty nest, Colleges and High School
and kids' first cars and all things little league, as my legs quiver and
my back feels like it will snap.

There's a box at the far end loaded to overflow with skateboards
and dirt bikes, bibs and cribs, first house, new job, first car and
bride.

I'm too tired to remember what it felt like to be twenty-something.

The Ayes Have It

I watch her from the patio doorway.
With her back to me, she stands in the middle of the party
crowd shoulder to profile with mister eye candy.
He lowers his chin and offers a phrase or two. Her head tilts
toward his, she brushes her hair and holds it behind her ear,
turns and smiles.
He smiles.
I know, an agreement has been reached.

Familiar

Sunglasses inverted
where you always
leave them

Sometimes a glimpse
catch of breath
almost a smile

A touch
back of the hand
more

Eight

I am the number 8.
To some, a simple two times four, but laid on edge,
I am infinity, the symbol of endlessness,
profligate of the innumerable,
boundless.

Viewed supine, I refuse containment,
burst spherically in a blur of immeasurable possibility,
true paradox of before, during, and after,
existing at once.

I bring shock to any who rely solely
on flat dependence of one two three
as guide to order, cadence of step, or compass and track;
chagrin to those surprised by disorder or misstep created
by my fertile, unexpected perspective.

Pray for My Brother

His world was growing smaller with each sunset.
The concrete bunk was brittle hard and cold on his seat
as snippets of many yesterdays skipped in and out of his consciousness.

Interloping clamor in adjoining cells tripped the shutter of his mind's eye
making it even more difficult to concentrate on just a single thought.
Memory darted from image to image in a splice of life montage.

He was alone in a sea of distractions.
Longing to regain comforts of family, fighting to harvest one good moment,
the hollow faced prisoner clasped his hands over his ears.

He waited, and listened for just the right signal to get strong enough
to bathe him in the private euphoria of good times remembered.
He failed, leaned back upon a windowless wall, and wept.

R. Martin Basden

Lost Along the Way

Where once a wooden cart bridge creaked
beneath the clop of hoof and groan of iron wheels
a mighty steel span of broader width provides
the modern transport ample way
from field to market and back
When everybody knew their way to church or mill or store
by passage across the little creek bridge
there was no need of signs
no need of arrows or distances to what lay beyond
cautions of right-of-way or warnings of high water
danger of ice on the bridge or bicycles or pedestrians
For the pace was pedestrian
a lifestyle unrushed
metered by sunrise and dusk
by seasons and weather
by traditions grounded in family
neighbors and community

A Meal at the Chrysler Museum

A feast set upon pedestal and canvas,
a repast that no king past or living
could imagine as fare for the masses,
is for us, right at hand.

Aperitif of glass twisted while hot
reaches for sunlight's lingering,
crimson bone inside a crystal arm
with fingerless palm.

Salad of everyday discards glued to wallboard,
varsity hues with clues in text revealing
violence, and anger, and revolt,
without a raised fist.

Side of tree, chisel formed.
Folded legs of a pregnant Madonna kneeling,
caressing her own smooth belly
with work worn hands.

Entree of creamy alabaster sculpted.
Christ's uplifted face to Father imploring,
while mankind held at bay
with just an upturned hand.

Dessert of trick photography.
Small pig held in a woman's arms,
her eyes and his follow you past their station
as she points seemingly to the exit.

Reconstruction

Retirement has become a search for ways to use leftovers. Not the half pastrami sandwich from too much lunch. Not the Tuesday list of tasks carried over from Monday. It's the serious business of making something whole from the fragments of life's interruptions.
We joke about what we might do when we grow up, but how does one actually engage the challenge to be meaningfully useful?
Where do you begin?
Groping for self near life's end finds an absolute parallel to the interminable brevity of adolescence.
The childhood freedoms lost in pursuit of test scores are elusive, and when glimpsed, play hide-and-seek as though embarrassed to be associated with wrinkles and sagging flesh.
No longer suffering the mundane urgency of earning a living, the discomfort becomes finding a life.
The anxieties of parenthood are not relieved by an empty nest, when you realize that you did make mistakes raising children.
Trying to compensate as a grandparent yields wonderfully incomplete rewards.
Losing a loved one, a friend, a job, a pet, or your favorite possession, only prepares one for tolerance to adversity, and offer slippery purchase as positive footholds in your new climb.
So, what to do?
Inventory the things you do well, and do them. Know your limitations. If you are a giver, keep giving. If you are a taker, consider a sweeping 180. Use your gifts and talents to make yourself and those about you glad that you are there. Accept love. Give it back. Keep sucking air. The rest is not up to you.

Broken
Haiku of injured relationship

Small pieces rattle
In the hollow of my mind
Of the whole once ours

R. Martin Basden

After Conflict

Burst against a closed door
shards of crystal
spears from goblet
litter the floor

I've had enough
struggled to keep the peace
strangled on censored wishes
unheard complaints

So now alone
why am I draped in regret
blanket of remorse
reward for being right

Conscience

There is a voice come to whisper
fragments of songs to a distracted heart

Offering good gifts unearned
purse from evil hard purchased

Often dismissed often ignored
the prick of it stirs you

Though you slumber eyes wide open
though you protest in your sleep

Parallels

Half the world in shadow
a natural thing as regular as sunrise
sure as the night
plainly visible

Half my heart in shadow
a natural thing for family separations
sure as the air
hardly visible

Practically identical

Roasting Regrets

I no longer have to choose between
my son's game and working late
or my girl's recital and overtime
They left home and left me to realize
I cheated myself
of precious moments to give to them
I no longer play family against employer
in the no-win trade of time for missed memories

Years of paying for absentee boarders followed
filled with the anxiety of no daily contact
burdening me with a sense of doors closing

It slowed my pace

With hope that retirement offered renewal
opportunity to do penance through grandchildren
I rushed to that juncture with pockets full of extra minutes
but they live days away
their parents busy
providing for them
and I count idle time
like loose change in an unused ashtray

R. Martin Basden

No Safe Passage (A Critique of Alzheimer's)

Habits that defined him every day
got brushed over
with strokes so slight
that purpose barely wobbled in its track
Comical at first
as we witnessed
surprise turn to dismay in him
humor turn to concern in us

He lost himself

Gone traditional dinner-time banter
replaced by onerous repetition
replaced by silence
Gone the familiarity of his unique personality
the captain now a hesitant mime
and worse
his treasonous body adds loss to loss
Strong upright posture
to rounded shoulder stoop
his trademark left-handedness
with pen and spoon
useless

The pace from walking to
just sitting
completed overnight
over years

He
does not live here now

Apathy or Fear

I stand as the blind and deaf pedestrian
among the rush of oncoming traffic
paralyzed by the near misses of weighty things blowing past
with such ferocity as to ruffle my clothing
certain that to remain stationary
condemns me to inevitable impact from variation of flow
certain that taking a step
will place me immediately in another flight path
certain that if nothing is done
something will happen

Checking the Obituaries

Checking the Obituaries
every morning
for peers
or strangers with familiar names
or age in my decade
or cause of death
or any similarity
to tie them to me
anticipating inevitability
happily surprised
I'm not there

Interruption

The muse drags me
from rut to rut
with careless regard
for my current comfort

Deaf to an objection
of not quite finished
she bribes me
with easy familiarity
that something much better
requires my attention

And with a finger tip
silences my complaint
points to a cache
of virginal phrases
promising
to name them
tomorrow

New Old Words

My ear is always tuned to vocabulary
which is why attention drifted
drew me from conversation
interrupted your discourse
branded me rude

I couldn't help it

Eclectic expression dimmed the light
of your magnetic being in mid-sentence
as a young man walked past
commented about the woofer and the Hottie
and suddenly I realized
the reference to an old dog was me

Singing is Praying Twice

To take the stage and share
the gift of song
artist and audience
may sample sublime
when music sets the pace
marks its own path
creates purpose above lyrics
impact beyond expectation

R. Martin Basden

A Peculiar Habit, Listening to Walls

Taunted from sleep
a disturbance almost repetitive somewhere in the house
drew me upright up barefoot to investigate in the dark

It wasn't the icemaker dumping new cubes
not the dog snoring or the ceiling fan's wobble
no doors ajar no windows open
something inside

From room to room
I placed my ear flat against the wall
listened for scratching or footsteps

Nothing but an indistinguishable hum
punctuated by irregular clicks and ticks

Back to bed and glad that the lights were all
off

Had I Only Known

I often think of the what ifs
couched in the when
of another time

Had it been possible
to finish the third before
seeing the first
it could have made
the would have done
less apologetic
less

had I only known

Boss Tom

I sat in the shade of a tree that hot August day
sippin' a Coke an' catchin' a breath from lawn work
when I saw that cat creepin' like I never saw him before
all hunkered down alongside a hedge
watchin' this big gray squirrel

It was like watchin' the movies
where the lion stalks his prey
only it was real and close
and in miniature

The big buck squirrel was king of his domain
havin' run off all the other smaller bucks
Boss Tom in his thick orange pelt
was unchallenged as feline ruler
even the dogs gave him a wide berth

He knew that cat was nearby
as he sat erect ten feet from the base of a huge pine
huskin' a cone for seeds
glancin' occasionally left and right
over his shoulders

Boss Tom was stretched out slinkin' in the grass
using that large pine tree to shield his approach
for what I'm sure he thought would be
a surprise attack

It wasn't

No sooner was the orange blur airborne
when a gray rocket hit him in mid-flight

Fur flew in tufts of gray and orange
from the livin' ball of fury rollin' about the yard
accompanied by yeowellin' an' snappin' an' sounds
not normal to either beast for every tick of
five seconds when bad boy pussy made a hasty exit
before all of the fur could settle to the ground
leavin' Mr. Gray to preen himself in leisurely fashion
sweepin' the last remnants of orange
from mouth and paw

Elegy for a Young Friend

It cannot be so easy to put into words
the measure of loss that steals breath at the news of your death.
No matter that vanguard couriers bore presage of decline
in numerous conflicting packets of hope and harm.
The sheer finality of it turned time inside-out
in a backward collage of last laugh, favorite places,
and shared moments, in a hide-and-seek rush
to capture every memory.
And we who will follow you
struggle to insulate ourselves
in this cavernous moment
with the warmth that was you.

Some Never Grow Up

It took some time to appreciate how I once made choices
Anything to avoid discomfort
Anyway to escape criticism
Everything to get my way

Cheeks stuffed with childhood sweetness never added weight
Friends' and siblings' disappointments rarely slowed me down
My birth family expected me to work for my keep
I left the human race at age thirteen
abducted I think by aliens for ten years
while my viewpoint changed

Homeless living in our parks
Honeybees no longer visit clover
Children with no safe playground
Bull-frog absent from the marsh
Not enough food in Korea
Fish die at the river mouth

News channels proliferate
Ignorance propagates
It is all related
Past Due notices have been issued
One can make a difference

Wisteria

For decades I have climbed this live oak
she with her stout horizontal limbs
defying gravity with outstretched arms
strong stoic solid
daring storms to wrest from her
the classic pose she has held for fifty years
and I in half that time have grown from seedling to menace
by ruse of gorgeous purple clusters of flowers hanging like
grapes
I've curried favor from the arborist
while steady in my purpose hoisted myself
 in sinuous twists girdling trunk and branch
First as tender vine I used her strength to support my growth
now as thick as she in the upper branches
my broad leaves compete for the same sunlight
my roots rob her of water and nutrients
As I get stronger life is choked from her until she fails
Soon I shall hug her skeleton
whose decay will feed me
to stand finally
on my own

Four Poets in Morning

Four poets in morning sit on compass points
Kneading words needing meaning
As wish memory and regret
Jostle for primacy

Control Issues

                    "Honey I'm home!"
No Answer, no cold beer in a frosted mug. I
busted ass to get home early,
Before the NFL drafts begin.
It's dark in here.
                    "Hey Babe, where are 'ya?"
Kitchen's too clean,
Guess she's picking up take-out.
No beer in the fridge, none in the garage.
                    "What the hell?"
I'll just crash in front of the TV.
Where's the remote?
Great! Got on all the lights,
Looked under every cushion.
                    "Where is that *#%& thing?"
Doorbell? The Pizza guy?
                    "I didn't order this!"
                    "My wife did?"
                    "What note?"

Out with the girls
One warm beer in your closet
Hope you like anchovies
I have the remote
Be in late
We'll talk

Sacrifice

No one can see the broken clasps on her bra
the pulled elastic of her panties
Friends know her coupon obsession
the bargain sale attendance record
her near passion for new bean and rice dishes
People notice her habit of wearing
the same outfit three days running
always clean and pressed
Everyone knows her smile
her soft voice
her strong concern for others
Her secret donations to charity
still secret

Back to Bed

Back to bed
for that wonderful cascade
across my shoulders
of sheet and blanket
back to the curling search
of dreams unfinished sliding
into the quiet darkness
of nowhere to be
right now

Motivation

Still moving sensation
even though standing still

I am home

to lay down my worries
for the day has been long
without pause to refresh or
reflect on the why of my trials

Softly a chortle from the dark
babbles and beckons me closer
To find her in faint light

My image
clear to her
who calls out singing now
song of why

R. Martin Basden

A Slice of Life

In premature staccato
half-intended snipe
leapt from my mouth
while my mind spun
like an empty movie reel

Before too-quickly spoken words
actually struck your ears
your eyes told me
you had read me
and knew the message

Of Sound Mind and Body

I witnessed his decline from shuffle to wobbly
wobbly to stagger
willing his failing body
next step next step
pulling his diminished frame erect beneath a toothless grin

Those beyond earshot turned pathos masks toward him
as he spiked the ground with his cane and flailed
his free arm to grasp elusive balance

Those in his presence were blessed with boundless positives
wit quick in gentle conversation
disengaging communicants from their prejudices

I witnessed her progress from wobbly to uniform
uniform to normal
repairing a failed body
therapy rote therapy
strengthening flesh and sinew

Those beyond earshot smiled at her cheerful countenance
as she padded relentlessly the endless belt
pumping arms in rhythm to imaginary march

Those in her presence were numbed by the absence
of timely responses and answers offered to unasked questions
disengaging herself from the genuine concern of communicants

I witnessed my step a bit wobbly today

R. Martin Basden

And for Everything a Season

Watching springtime come, someone in my stead kept vigil over my
early days;
pruned my tender branches, molded my growth, nourished, cared for,
loved me.

With eyes scarcely opened I almost remember watching my spring
depart,
watching summer come.

Alive with the all seeing, little understanding, joy of youth;
all hearing, all feeling and utterly unaware
of other seasons.

How long the summer!
My warmest days seem numberless and without bounds.

And so it has been, my unmemorable spring, my glorious summer,
were someone else's summer and fall,
and I never knew it.

How to suddenly understand what has always been,
recalling now the subtleties of preceding, overlapping, following
seasons.

Autumnal vestiges remain like a mantle on forebear's hibernal coat.
I missed their fall, and only this instant is vesper's presence
acknowledged.

Still in my summer I understand the unevenness of human seasons,
And through other's winter see my approaching fall.

I shall enjoy all of this.

Why Is It Called Farewell?

All afternoon I have been struggling
how to tell you goodbye

We have been riding now for hours I suppose
my silence could say something
somehow speak my discomfort of this intersection
this crossroads we inhabit for a moment

Strange how but a blink among eons can take so long
take such weighted toll in the choice one must make
when years are a blur and a single thought covers it all
It has been good

You have been my faithful companion
and I am a coward to let the Veterinarian
do my job

Happily Ever After

I do not think the ending can be right
left the way it is
with its practiced forgone conclusion

After all
in the wizardry of current technology
it's a simple task to add new interaction
to bend the story line mid-stream
put in suspicion without revelation

Skip the salacious sex scene as a quadriplegic
plots revenge on his cheating wife
Let the lost puppy grow up
hunt people in the woods
anything but same old same old

I would sooner wrap my mind
around the smell of purple nines
juggling limes in a dark corner of the sun
than trade surprise for redundancy

When Morning Comes

I faint would know the day nor recognize the hour
but for the shadows cast upon the west wall
For having run full out and breathless laid me down
to find refreshment it sleep's bosom
begin to rouse
and stirring to the absence of my spouse in bed
my struggle just to wake
puts me to sleep again

To dream those half-real scenes which haunt my waking
For not to know if they are true or tangled messages
of times past or times future
whose faces are at once familiar and unknown
and deeds confusing in their twisted version of near reality
the taste and smell of which remains so very palpable
they cause my lids to rise
when morning comes

The Dog Smiles at Me

The dog smiles at me,
sits upright, front legs raised, paws dangling as if disjointed,
begs for a walk in the freakish cold winds of March.

She feigns patience, as a second sweater, hooded jersey,
ear muffs, ski mask, gloves, and jacket are pulled, tucked,
zipped, and stretched over an already well insulated body.

Her smile broadens
when the leash, her signal to the door, is clipped to collar.

The insufficiency of such restraint is immediate
as twenty pounds of hound drags more than ten times her weight
to twenty seven pee stations in eight blocks.

Perhaps she wasn't smiling.
Maybe it was a grimace
from a full bladder.

Absence

I have not sat in so much nearby quiet
while distant clatter invites attendance
yet the taking of this moment necessary
in a dark corner of this lighted room
as I contemplate when
you might smile at me again

R. Martin Basden

Scoundrel

Where were you
as the howling beast of neglect
ran me down
and savage had his way?
You, with no time
for trophy children,
tossed responsibility weightless
to whatever breeze happened by.
Me, relegated to all things necessary,
toil to care for our babies,
mewling in shades of want.

The we that was, is done.

The we who wait
rely upon one who will not curse you,
who cannot forgive you,
who lives in the rhetorical why.

Out

Do not presume my favor or rely on my shoulder
as from that very perch you slurred
betrayed counsel given in trust

Mine the blame
for mistaking hubris for self-confidence
facility of tongue as worthiness

Yours the burden of loneliness in the crowd
who will notice that you are no longer
my friend

R. Martin Basden

The Fly Fisherman

As expected, there was no breeze
no ripple
in the water

Alone

With hand tied lure,
the latest in waders,
the newest in rod and line,
I stepped into coolness up to my shins and began
the art of a practiced skill

As wrists flexed and fingers played the line
swishing back and forth
the sound whispering encouragement
to make the perfect cast
the cast that would snag the trophy
the trophy that would cast me as
Champion

Increasing the back and forth
imagining the crowds calling my name
I was about to . . .

when a crash caused my shoulders to jump for my ears
and frozen in mid-stroke
line looping over hat brim
I turned to see
my six-year-old
staring at a fully dressed fisherman
standing in a bathtub

An Awkward Pause

The things I have not said hang
in the yeast of silence brewing
something unrecognizable.

Bitter words aged mellow, hint
of their raw poison efficacy,
retain the sorry taste of hate.

A compliment withheld,
humor unshared,
love untold, rot
to untouchable recovery, each
sacrificed on procrastination's altar,
look and smell the same.

Bitter Spring

Bitter spring in floral skirt
how imprecise your promise.
How quick you turn away as winter claims late
a bargain you surely forgot you made with him
and give but a glimpse of sunshine
before an Easter snow.

Don't think your winsome smile and coy pirouette
can make amends for youthful disregard of calendar,
nor hope that we will not remember your sisters
who brought a proper waltz to their season.

Sweep with your arms warm winds before you,
leap through their coils in joyful rush,
to wake the torpid world.

Temporary Jewel

Tiny droplet of dew gliding slowly to pause
at the tip of a slender leaf.
Waiting for inevitable gravity,
the jewel swells, then slips
to the very point of the downturned perch.
There it hangs, quivering,
rainbows dancing within as the morning sun
pierces the now elongated pear shaped form.
A gleaming crystal shimmering with life
borrowed for a moment from its host.
Suddenly gone, its only trace
The gently bobbing of a now lighter
blade of grass.

From the Heart

How often we say it's from the heart,
as if invocation gives dispensation
for the havoc wrought by words,
like no hammered steel
or whetted edge can cause.

Righteous in anger, prejudice, or revenge,
weapons of smoke, pierce
where fingers cannot touch,
cut, where fragile hope resides.

And have we forgot as they,
we are pitiable creatures,
tugging ribbons of self respect
to hide wide gashes
suffered in similar manner?

Beyond

Beyond the reach of clarity
faint timbre
like the tap and scrape of a dried leaf on a window
or faintest whistle of air
through a distant crevice
more tease than tell
more distraction than revelation
makes me turn my head
strain for its source
the near voice-like quality I imagine

R. Martin Basden

Faithful Is the Man

It has not gone unnoticed
the way of your path among us
though you may have wished it so at times

By your selfless dedication
you have not hidden among us well
for someone here knows the loving son
who gave care in his Mother's dotage
as all faithful sons should do
and shared with us your tasks

By your self-effacing demeanor
you failed to be unseen
for someone here knows the willing churchman
who served committees, and more
as all faithful parishioners should do
and shared with us your knowledge

By your very quietness you are known
for someone here knows the constant worker
who raked the leaves, scrambled eggs, and more
as all faithful followers should do
and shared with us your labors

By your very faithfulness you are known
for someone here knows the dedicated family man
who chose well for his wife and children
as all faithful men should do
and shared with us your pains and joys

Now go in faith as you are known
for someone here knows more about the faithful man
who quietly gave an apostolic helping hand
as all faithful apostles should do
and later may share with us your memorable good

Before the Bench

From a distance it was hard to tell male or female
of the form huddled alone on the park bench in morning light.
A closer step was needed to satisfy my curiosity.
An old man pulled a too small cardigan across his back,
struggled to make the buttons reach with hobbled fingers.
While moments for me were longer for him, he got two done,
and satisfied with the effort hinged himself sideways to lie down.
A wad of newsprint was his pillow; open pages became his covers
for another visitation to sleep. His eyes closed, his fisted hands
beneath his chin offered a picture of prayer on its side.

I stood awhile imagining his reverie.
A stream of thoughts, of times long passed, rocking in his mental
hammock?
Or maybe just a review of last night's brew and whatever passed
for chow,
held court in his mind, seeking an appeal, or at least a re-run.
Hard to tell.

Is there happiness after usefulness?

I Know He Carried Her
For the Mother of my Friend Nancy Kay

In the shadow of a raven on the wing
floats a gossamer image
an image of the fairest one
the fairest one I knew
Like a scarf below his wingbeats
as his wing beats drew
parting air to lift her shadow
to match his
'til they mingled
'til they parted
and the raven flew due West
while to the North
to the North and out of sight
she flew

Family Ties

Give me back the memory never earned
of times before I knew myself
and counted on parents
to tote my share
of family history
while I in careless play
from lazy morn to failing light
gave no thought to those who went before

Give me back such squandered days
of times when I only knew myself
so swollen by my self esteem
that all the universe
took pulse
or so it seemed
from this sole strapping soul
who took no breath for those whose breath was short

Give me back the stories told
of kin whose deeds were lost on me
as I listened but did not hear
and now can only grasp a vague sense
of who they were or how their lives
touched mine
as I busied myself through decades
and only stood the ceremony of dust to dust impatiently

Give me back the whole of life
for now I tire of me
and find how valuable the thread
that stitches patchwork lives into family quilts
now in my hand
and every tattered fiber I reclaim waits
the gathering which is my privilege to host
the honor of those gone to those coming

You Finally Made It

There comes the strangest moment in your life
as an edge of identity blurs a little
when consciousness forms an instant list

The way you point at your children
a phrase frequently repeated
crossing right ankle over left
the ritual of opening mail
lines at the corners of your eyes

cause a smile in the mirror
at your parent

Anxiety

Confluence of tinnitus and thought
thunders unsorted
into the confines of my waking

Left-over challenges and tasks
bumping against me
irritating yelping pups
begging satisfaction
dismissed again
as I attend the demands of
vague pervasive apprehensions

Durable Goods

They move among us, unselfish. They take little, give much,
do their job with minimum maintenance, time after time,
regardless of interruption or delay,
in spite of objection or critique,
underappreciated, ignored, perhaps slandered.

They work, they care, they love, when love is the only answer
for the deprived, the disenfranchised.
In place of family, instead of blood, they offer
concern beyond residence, advice above expectation.

They are the durable good, the lasting impression,
who bear the burden of an ever increasing need
to expunge ignorance, imbue tolerance,
give foundation for a lifetime of learning.

They are the durable good, the memory makers,
who show how to be a positive, contributing, citizen of the world.
The durable good, the teachers of our children.

Distracted

A moth landed on his hand
and in that moment
autism's veil fluttered
distant eyes focused
tiny feet tickled
soft wings pulsed
until he smiled

R. Martin Basden

Just a Stack of Syllables
(Four Short Unrelated Poems)

Talk of passion is a boat without tiller
driven by desire for warmth.
Fueled by imagination touching anticipation,
words whisper everything possible,
wander everywhere sensitive, until talk
is not enough.

~

What had November done but tease us
with morning shivers and midday sweats.
For choosing wool instead of cotton,
we tangle in the discards of poor planning.

~

They have been with us a long time and they're breeding.
The me first commanders on our roadways,
folks who hold meetings in doorways,
theatre talkers who never learned to whisper,
vandals, litterbugs, ninety-decibel radio freaks;
takers, who steal from themselves the gift of giving.

~

He would declare and could himself believe himself to be a poet
except
that verbosity overtakes his intentions to purify a single thought,
multiplies with unfettered glee splashing
in a stream of consciousness
too long for memoir, too short for novelette,
smothering his attempt to do justice
to just one line.

Fear of Crying

We don the necktie or boots, carry briefcase or hand tools,
forge path through difficulty imposed between goals and
intent, struggle to give meaning to our life, and spend great
effort to hide evidence that we are no different one from the
other.

How useless that hardened disguise to one 's self when life
offers proof of universal necessities, commands acceptance
of our humanity, demands compliance, howsoever reluctantly
given.

How vulnerable the beast heart beats beneath sinew and
layered cloak, faux protection from the thrust of love's
piercing stare, or the serrated edge of demeaning
monologue.

How delicate the covering that men put around themselves
as armor against compliment and criticism, both of which
rend the fiber, lend the tender secret of emotion exposed to
unwanted scrutiny.

Later, Maybe

In the shadows of a lifetime, wait the unfinished, the
interrupted interests put aside by distraction, hard choices, or
decision by indecision.

Like old men in ragged trousers, hands shoved deep into
pockets, stir dust with the sole of one shoe, they wait.

Resignation in their countenance, hesitation in their whispers,
they scheme on how to gain my attention, and draw straws
for assignment.

Perhaps today a swatch of color, or the way laughter hangs in
air will prompt a reach for the gate latch of memory, will give
impetus to a hesitation of routine.

Finally, time to test the waters, stretch myself, grab the
should-haves, the could-haves, or maybe,
tomorrow.

Sully 444
of my friend, accompanist, Maestro Bobby Sullivan

You turned your head
but for a moment and half
a life was spent
children now parents
passion now comfort

Where did the moment go full
of hours at work crammed
with frenetic creation
the music
the schedule
the hope of value
in the spending of it

Thirty years come to this breath
this taking in of breath
to taste how beauty has been wrought
what threads woven binding you
to all you have touched

For we the wordless couriers
of a scoreless song
of a poem unwritten
hum the harmony
to your melody
and listen
for a change in key

Martha's Harvest

Martha had buried the woman's name twenty years ago;
smothered in rich layers of life, no hint of resurrection.
Now, in genteel conversation
a fetid offering placed innocently before her,
the name took immediate currency.
Surging recognition pinched Martha's shoulders
as revisited anger stiffened her
and a litany of ancient wrongs
hung from rusted blades
plunged into her back
by that woman
years ago.

In the roaring silence of her own reverie she became aware
of the courier offering a second message.
The name's owner has cancer
and is near end

The winds of rage fell silent.
in the new quiet, she prayed.

Guided by a sure strong hand
she sought her out
and somehow found words
she had not prepared
which healed both their wounds
and she buried anger with her

Spring is a Love-Hate Season

Fields of jonquils and daffodils
tout their sun and butter faces
in the glow of first light.
Sweet hyacinth
stationed in royal clusters
along the garden path
capture the senses
reward the search
with sights and smells
and nostrils full of pollen

Pine and oak sprinkle the finest gold
dust on every surface
hope of new life
viewed through red eyes
accompanied by trumpeting
sneezes and the honking
of runny nose

Weeding Is Forever

The sound of children at play in the neighborhood yards,
a delight to my ear on these balmy spring afternoons.
I bask in the sun's warmth,
almost aware of a faint breeze
rippling the hair on my arm
as the latest Organic Gardener issue
folds itself shut in my lap.
A sense of everything in its season, all in its place,
trees budding, bulbs in bloom, wild onions
already twice the height of the lawn.

Oh crap!
I forgot the pre-emergence application.
I'm numbed that it's too late for treatment.
I'll have to weed.

No matter that all the veggies and flowers are greenhouse
grown,
that the planting area is raked and picked clear of every stem
and root,
dormant weed seeds are exposed, and the battle begins.

Don the gloves and floppy hat, grab the trowel,
step out with pail and kneeling pad in hand.
Hours bent to the task,
stiff from the up and down,
pail overflowing when time to quit,
but I know:
The plucking of each weed looses still more dormant spores.
Those with hardy roots, regenerate from remnants of flesh
left in the soil.
Air joins the fray to dust interlopers at the very feet of my
desirables.
Even the family pet sloughs fur-borne contaminants with a
stroll nearby.

And, as I struggle to right myself,
a new weed winks at me
between smiling pansies.

Gift of Interruption

Familiar words in an unusual clump
crowd the casual oblivion of my path
distractions become revelation
as they arrange themselves
not by length but heft
and offer new usefulness

Shuffle quickens to saunter
ostentation gets gaudy
angry stays pissed
sad morphs to morose
interruption is inspiration

Clean Slate

Waiting for sunrise at a ritual place
as wrinkles of darkness glow with a hint
that the moment is near
when a burning curve will blossom
beneath an awning of clouds
spill itself
toward this spot
warm my face and heart
and burn yesterday's sorrows
in the promise of new beginnings

I Have Reason to Smile

I have reason to smile,
though I find it difficult to sit upright
now that stuffing has been lost.
You were my first.
What wonderful nights we spent together,
your head resting on my belly.
I remember the very day you discovered my eyes,
the fascination on your soft features,
first a poke, then a twist, later a taste.
You especially liked my left flipper,
moist from mouthing,
nibbling until you fell to sleep.
What fun we had at mealtimes,
refusing those horrid creamed peas.
We took baths together after an escape
to the soil of a new garden, always good for a laugh.
Those romps on the staircase; stomp and count going up,
slide down screaming.
What memories!
And now, you're gone.
I watch, I wait,
I have reason to smile.

Christening the New House

It would have been wonderful
except
while we slept on the third floor
a toilet overflowed
during the night
on the first floor
of our new home
created a river over the tile foyer
which became a waterfall in the garage
spread across the delta of the two-car expanse
soaked boxes awaiting room assignment
wicked God knows what
into Lord only knows
hidden inside

Anger Aside

For a moment
I took a person's life

As surely as honed steel between arms
thrown up in defense
unable to parry decibel blows

Fierce phrases intending harm
inflicted damage through the useless filters
of hands cupped over ears

I screamed

Pounded fear by mouthfuls in a crushing rage
on a bowed head
until I heard myself strangle on half a word
and quit

Knowing
a lifetime of apology
will not repair
my harm

If One Could Write

Balanced on the edge of sleep
when din of strident day slows to contain itself
when quiet wraps the soul in certain peace
a voice whispers miracles in imagery
calling for memory to cast a gentle net
beneath a flow of beauty
pouring stories begging to be told
spoken in exquisite phrase
words of truth

Soon comes the dawn
dressed like Mardi Gras
announced with zydeco
to shoo away catalogued grandeur
make discovery play hide-and-seek
among masked faces
dancing out of sight
which look nothing
like the truth

Harbinger

She's ninety-four
telling me about talking to her Mama
Says she can't make out what Mama says
but it must be important
it sounds the same every time
I tell her it's because one of them is deaf
the other dead for forty years
She stares out the window
pushes a tear with the back of her hand
and mouths a silent response

Molly Sings

A song that we each know
lingers in memory's fickle play
day by day a melody
of maddening repetition
in differing key and unmatched lyric
sometimes ballad sometimes march
seldom quite complete

Before we hear it we're humming
cadence to mundane tasks
welcome distraction to boredom
interloper of purpose
irresistibly we hum
a song that we each know

Hammer or Shoes

What wakes me in so dark an hour?
Three or four spins of the hand
have spent my allotment for this night,
tossed me restless upon thin membranes of tasks
in need of conclusion without definition of solution.
We are remodeling a house.
The simplicity of demolition, reconstruction, and occupation
vaporizes with the application of schedule, change, and delay.
We are held hostage by the necessities of priority evolution
due to recalcitrant workmen, changes in work definition,
and re-work caused by the smallest of water leaks
defying revelation.
I wonder what remodeling meant to the caveman?
Would he chisel a new bed platform for a growing family,
roll a boulder from one side to the other
to meet his *Feng Shue*, or simply trudge off
to find another hole in the hillside?

Negotiation

What is this madness called compromise
that steals desire with a promise of peace?
When one spirit is quenched
to brittle inflexibility
in the bath of another's cold oil,
one stands superior,
the other kneels,
defenseless.

Rather, let there be combat,
not to death, but to clear victory,
as skill and ardor clash
so order is defined.
Then let grace command the victor
lift the contestant by his side
to stand not as vanquished,
but as worthy.

Last Summer

There was a time when the entire world was a shoreline.
I would spend my summers there as a child.
Nothing was ever hot like the sand, which required
a ritual approach to the ocean.

Brisk walk up spare shade of dunes,
dead run down the sunny side and
sprint across shifting blistering misery,
to hurl oneself into shocking blue-green chill.
It would take your breath away,
but your feet didn't care.

Ahhh, summer!
floating on my back in the ocean,
pleasant coolness tickled my belly,
sun toasting face to form crow's feet at squint lines.
I would glow red for an hour or two
by evening sport new tan over old
in the blush reserved for youth.

Perspectives

There was time to lie out, catch some rays,
shoot the breeze with friends, or sleep on the beach.
Time to daydream, catalog faces or forms
in the summer issue of cloud billows,
name the dunes made to look like
neck-less heads of balding men by the wind.
Or, let your imagination really run wild,
looking at a favored treat, dressed
in a lot less than school clothes.

Hello? Summer? Where have you gone? I don't recall your
leaving.

But, now I'm here, and you were then, and I remember you.

R. Martin Basden

That's Not Funny

Running late for a meeting
noticed a snagged thread on my left sleeve
found scissors in a kitchen drawer
slipped thumb and two fingers into handles
realized they were my wife's small left-handed pair

Made vain attempts to cut but
blades didn't shear
grabbed instead
locking scissors to sleeve and worse
my large right thumb stuck

Panic ensued
sought assistance room to room
found her on the back porch
headsets on

She looked up
smiled
and laughed

Estrangement

Waiting for a call
like so many times before
it may not come
it will not come
on any schedule I may concoct
to salve wounds
or simply hear familiarity

It might be a text
a cold cluster of letters
wrought to resemble loving contact
without touch without breath without life
and it may not come

Verdant Deception

Abrogation of truth
Crouches among full hedgerows
Of hypocrisy, patriotism,
And oversold success

Behind the façade
Of State controlled Free Press
Visas are denied
To journalists and reporters
Those blue collar poets
And white collar psalmists
Forbidden opportunity
Of challenge
By word and photograph
Forbidden entry
As levelers of veracity
Feared by the gate keepers
Of kingdoms large and small

From the banks of Zambezi
To the banks of Zurich
From the steppes of Caucasus
To the steps of Congress
All roads in the light of truth
Lead to hope
Unless
Traffic is detoured
And shunted into darkness
While the storerooms of opportunity
Are looted by the flagmen

A war is started
Based upon third hand rumors
From too many twice paid advisors
As a distraction
From the collapse of money palaces
Where the acid rain of ruin
Beats harsh upon the naked head

Of countless voiceless thousands
Impaled upon the gaff
Of caveat emptor
While gilded umbrellas
Cover CEOs
Of kingdoms large and small

Simplistic in practice
Far from simple
Red blossoms of lies
Bloom freely
On the new green vine
Of deception
In kingdoms large and small

Sorry

An insincere apology
rattles in the ear
as harsh as that
which begs its necessity.

Town and Country Linda

We expected
a heavy chocolate woman, the poet,
perhaps in unmatched recycle,
dark hair bracketing a round shiny face.
She peddled painful testimony
of backwoods Arkansas, in the dialect of poverty,
swabbed in indelible misery that seemed
her wage and her regret.
Had us
pricking fingertips red on cotton bolls,
witnessing a stillbirth, trying to ignore
hunger pangs and the uselessness of complaint.

So much anguish
from the well dressed, size three bundle of erudite whiteness
that hiked all five feet of her into our place
to claim authorship.

Take a Pass

With but a handshake
a paragraph of conversation
a hand-full of eye contacts
the aroma of expectation
took my breath

How can one know the other's thoughts
but watch the language of movement
the lack of negatives the hint of positives
hidden in public verbiage

Weighing I and You
searching for We
I chose the ambiguity of parting
before sharing could turn
warming fantasy
into cold reality

Suspicion

You took a walk and came back here smiling
color in your cheeks and hair tossed back
gone just enough so I would not be worried
about the noticed break in your routine

What in the world has made you look so happy
the glow you have emitting love so strong
just close enough to see that you've changed
too far away to understand

Shall I remain as silent in my worry
as you in your unwillingness to share
should I try to slow you from your hurry
risk a greater separation

Answers to my questions never spoken
may contain sharp edges of despair
awaiting voluntary words of explanation
I turn my head and look away

Letter Unsent

Once again the storm has come pretending as my friend
to softly pound intrusive stuff upon my last defense,
and by an almost unobtrusive method steals my wind,
then slips away by newborn breach of our communal fence.

In fury have I torn the words from rubble in my heart,
and choked on countless vicious thoughts congealed,
so not to have the breath or strength to verbalize my part
as brooding silence screams a lie concealed.

To wrestle with the you and I, I cast myself alone,
committing random tumbling thoughts upon a folded page,
and fondle each and every one right through the flesh to
bone,
to find what's real and meaningful and throw away my rage.

When done, the letter pages long, contains my very soul,
and yet, my spirit calmer now, is resting, having spent
my anger without hurting you, I've satisfied my goal,
catharsis more than weaponry is the letter sealed unsent.

Stream of Consciousness

Take me to a place of escape
where calls for my attention can be ignored
Take me to a place of timeless comfort
to drift between quiet and acute awareness of surroundings
oblivious to history and rote
where fresh and new abound and wonder rediscovered
dwells
a place where reality and fantasy are twins hand-in-hand
in a mirrored world and I a welcomed companion
may walk with them

There I shall fill my pockets with creative seeds
and harvest ideas in great profusion into satchels
fare for later consideration and if
I come upon something original I pray
that it shall be wrapped in such protective shield
to preserve innocence until
the muse and I dress it appropriately
for a very proper cotillion

Mark the Date

Remember the swell of mystery,
the Oh My God wonder of childbirth concluded,
most to be celebrated in annual ribbon ritual
unless,
the first few are the last
breaths.

Remember the sweep of anguish,
the Oh My God wonder of what and why,
of harsh circumstance delivered
in lieu
of pink or blue
expectations.

Siblings

When you had three sisters,
the prize for being first at the morning table
was your choice of
the best that Mom cooked,
the last of the sugar corn flakes,
or the biggest breakfast pastry.
The penalty, however,
for trading first at chow for last in the bathroom
was a cold shower.

When the odds were three to one,
veracity provided little shelter
against mewling connivance,
that charged the older brother
guilty by show of hands.

When one considers siblings:
for all the shoving and teasing
laughing and crying
hurting and healing
it was better than growing up
an only child.

Opossum in the Headlights

I want to get to the other side
just make passage
and be on my way
No protest planned
No agenda touting traffic control
I'll slide into the woods and vanish
You'll probably never see me again
unless you intersect my path
by accident or intent
in which case
I'll change my name
take from you my smiling face
my comical wobble
lie here altered on the road
and on the altar of your memory

Sonnet for Prisoners

If I could change small snippets of my life
and set some awful wrongs I'd done aright,
to take away my victims' blameless strife,
then restful sleep might come to me tonight.
You've bound me by the law to make amends,
by jury vote for what you know I've done.
But mine, a prison no one comprehends,
a silent guilt where freedom's never won.
The wishes that repeat themselves each day,
for help in an impossible request,
to re-live all those instances and pray,
the bad times of the past are put to rest.
No matter if I reach for where it went
no matter, since the moment has been spent.

Today I Changed a Lightbulb

On days during and following chemo therapy my body is not
my own
Energy needed to do daily rituals is a most valued commodity
Simple walks from bed to kitchen to bathroom to den wear
me out
Those days of hours in the garden
taking long walks
working in the shop
are postponed
In my mind I rebuild garden fences
transplant crowded beds
dream designs for hand hewn wood carvings
target opportunities for priority activity
and speculate when I might have reserves enough to do
anything
The confluence of energy and opportunity are rare
In the tug between body and mind
the body wins
Today I changed a light bulb

Strung Up

Bent over his guitar
in the throes
of flying fingered crescendo
on a riff
so intense
strings vanished
in the tortured blur
of the moment

As one with the music
one with the instrument
lost
in his creation
until his beard
so carefully concealed
behind the guitar neck
joined uninvited
to mute the humming strings

and where
melodic chords had just departed

sotto voce
accapella
"OH!"

Missing Someone

Missing Someone
Is not a function of time
not a mere gathering of primary memories
It is instant and pervasive ritual
conceived in the hollow of absence
born in piteous darkness
groping for something not there

The forever pleasant voice
that would finish your sentence
rings its counsel and laughter
in the unstill corridors of your mind

And nobody can tell you how
to come to the light until
other pathways cross in grace
to sing new harmony
to your new melody

Still Life

The man sits with a timelessness
his grandfather kept
waiting for the moment
best suited for movement
for hoisting gun to shoulder
the practiced swing and squeeze
ahead of fleet wings startled
by the stump come to life
amid dry reeds which whispering no warning
in their casual touch and sway
no signal of deadly clamor
of smoke clearing
while dog fetches
and quiet settles on the pond
with a timelessness undisturbed

R. Martin Basden

The Burden of a Friend

They call me Doctor

It is not always within me to keep separate
the objectivity of profession and empathetic response
as clients become friends when
anonymity is lost to repetitious intimacies

The revelation of certain sacredness
drawn from the everyday
sustains me through times
when I must make humor from horror
to sometimes wear the countenance of a clown
and exaggerate my confidence
that one step up can make a large difference
for my friend who is wordlessly down

To do so without lying is a challenge

I have learned to make joyful the tiniest success
a banquet of the smallest morsel of hope
in a world of injury and despair
in the unforgiving steps of aging
or on the see-saw of cause and effect

For mine is the burden of a friend
someone to lighten what staggers the spirit
someone to help when there are more handles than hands

Shaving

On usual days I would not have noticed
soap scum and whisker-ends
floating in the bowl rushing
near the overflow
to a waterfall
out of sight

I would have ignored
tiny rafts of bubbles
unable to resist the pull
the spin of eddies
waiting their turn after
vanishing companions

Today these small things
offer sobering parallel
as I shave for the funeral
of a friend

The Neighborhood Watch

I heard the dogs before sirens
whined their way into the neighborhood.
Badges busted the kegger next door.

It hadn't been the noise of revelers,
not excess cars strewn about neighbor's yards,
the complaint.

Decency had been violated.

The longer the dance, the lighter the clothes.
A man with no pants, socks without shoes,
strolled through widow Creedy's yard,
and blew her a kiss.

I'm glad I left early.

Shadows

Shadows on my window on a dark and rainy night
can't make out the image as they fly
causes me to wander back in time when things were right
dries my throat and makes me want to cry

Echoes in my mind go by unnumbered as I pause
futile efforts mine exact a toll
in heartbeat felt, a lifetime spent, waiting for the cause
turn within myself to grip my soul

Did I see a day gone by in new perspective shown
followed by a task I've left undone
was it reason new revealed, a something I have known
pulls me back and makes me want to run

Could be something from my past, or something I desire
tests I've failed or one I'm yet to meet
give me less than I deserve or more than I require
kind in future, or in past discreet

Now I stand and tremble from the brief encounter free
still bewildered though I don't know why
guess I'll always wonder 'bout my past and what's to be
live for now and curse when shadows fly

R. Martin Basden

Short Cut

While driving
along a busy road
a snapshot
framed through the side window
just a glimpse
just enough to gain a sense
that old man and boy share reluctance
at the entry of a darkened alley

The cane
both prop and weapon
probes the sunless passage
hindered by a tiny fist
gathering clutches of sleeve as
in my rear view mirror they
disappear into the gloom
where shadows build hiding places
for fear

Rescue Words

There is no end, no beginning,
simply the middle of a poem.
You, the reader, must make assumptions,
find meaning among unfamiliar words,
tie your concept of origin to moral
disguised as conclusion or presented
as convenient stopping point
by a poet bent on impressing you
with something which could be powerful
if it fills a notch, completes a thought,
gives you a crevice to drive piton
that saves you.

About the Author

This great-grandfather has always been involved in creative endeavors: singer, humorist, engineer, landscaper, master gardener, youth soccer coach, leader of several community and fraternal organizations, and active churchman.

R. Martin Basden and his wife Kay have been married for 57 years, during which time they shared careers in real estate, business ownership, and raised 2 very successful children.

Although he has been writing for several decades, an interest in publication was encouraged by his beloved Albright Poets, 13 women with whom he shared editorial exercises. These ladies heckled and cajoled him into submitting his poetry for publication in the last decade or so.

Dozens of poems have been published individually at *vox poetica*, *Moondance*, *Camel Saloon*, *Cavalcade of Stars*, and *Tidewater Review*, and in several anthologies including *Carvings in Stone*, *Albright Anthology*. and others.

Publication Credits

Grateful acknowledgment is made to the following where some of the poems (or earlier versions) first appeared:

Camel Saloon: As if We Could Change Things

Jeanette Cheezum's Cavalcade of Stars: Good Morning, From the Tree I Used to Climb

vox poetica: Interruption, Distracted, No Safe Passage, I Have No Memory of Love, Broken (Haiku of Injured Relationship), Ode to Bob Christin, The Anchors of Our Lives, Durable Goods, Mark the Date, Sandy Hook Silence, A Likeness,

Other Titles Published by Unbound Content

Mothers Ought to Utter Only Niceties
A Bank Robber's Bad Luck With His Ex-Girlfriend
By KJ Hannah Greenberg

A Strange Frenzy
By Dom Gabrielli

Memory Chose a Woman's Body
By Angela M Carter

Our Locust Years
Before the Great Troubling
By Corey Mesler

Just Married
By Stan Galloway

Backwoods and Back Words
By Nicole Yurcaba

Riceland
By CL Bledsoe

In New Jersey
By Julie Ellinger Hunt

Inspiration 2 Smile
By Nate Spears

Painting Czeslawa Kwoka: Honoring Children of the Holocaust
By Theresa Senato Edwards and Lori Schreiner

Tongues in Trees
Wednesday
The Pomegranate Papers
This is how honey runs
By Cassie Premo Steele